Take a Deep Breath

# Take a Deep Breath

The Haiku Way to Inner Peace

Sylvia Forges-Ryan
Edward Ryan

the apocryphile press
BERKELEY, CA
www.apocryphile.org

apocryphile press
BERKELEY, CA

Apocryphile Press
1700 Shattuck Ave #81
Berkeley, CA 94709
www.apocryphile.org

First published by Kodansha America.
Copyright 2002 by Sylvia Forges-Ryan and Edward Ryan.
First Apocryphile edition, 2006.

ISBN 1-933993-07-3

Printed in the United States of America

Illustrations by Noriko Murotani.
Reprinted by permission of Kodansha International Ltd.

The translation of Basho's haiku on p. 17 is by
William J. Higginson (author of *The Haiku Handbook*),
and is used with his permission.

*To our daughter Susanna and our son Eric*

# C O N T E N T S

*In a Garden of Ten Thousand Flowers*

*We try to believe*
*the wide shawl*
*of the black*
*night sky*
*is stitched*
*with infinite*
*care and design.*

*We want to feel*
*in a garden of ten*
*thousand flowers*
*one life*
*means something*
*or anything*
*at all.*

*Some have found joy*
*in visions grand*
*as a celestial rose*

*or humble as heaven*
*in the palm of a hand.*

*But why this need*
*to elaborate*
*the mystery*
*of all that is?*

*Is it not enough*
*and more*
*to leave it all*
*unmetaphored?*
*To simply name*
*and let it*
*be.*

*As here*
*in this patch*
*of violets, in this stone*
*and in the encompassing*
*silence.*

# PREFACE

Stop now. Close your eyes. Take a deep breath. A *deep* breath—beginning right down in your abdomen and filling all the way up to your collarbone. And again. And now again. Three deep breaths. Now, relax. Gently and without judgment allow your attention to focus on the natural rhythm of your breath. Not on the thought "I am breathing" but on the *experience* of it. Whether in your nostrils, or at the back of your throat, or in your chest, or your abdomen, be aware of the breath as it comes in and goes out, as it rises and falls. Allow yourself to rest for a few moments in the breath. In and out, rising and falling. If your mind wanders, gently draw it back to your breathing. Rest in the awareness of the actual experience of it. Notice that no special effort is required. The breath breathes itself.

Allow yourself a few moments to do this.

Nothing we will say to you in this book will be as important as allowing yourself to stop now and do this.

Love yourself enough to stop and do this.

In just those few moments, you have had the basic experience of deep spiritual knowledge. You have allowed yourself to stop. You have brought your attention to your breath, to just your breath. And you have realized how inclined you are to do anything else but stop and pay attention.

That's all there is to enlightenment. Stopping. Paying attention to *just this*, whatever it may be. Realizing that the mind will go anywhere else— which is the nature of the mind. And discovering that it's possible, gently and without judgment, to come back to *just this*.

11

# INTRODUCTION

*Consider the lilies of the field. They toil not neither
do they spin. Yet I say to you that even Solomon in
all his glory was not arrayed like one of these.*

When we hear words like these we may think: what a wonderful insight!
I wish *I* could be as wise as that. But the truth is that, to see the glory of
those field lilies, all that's required is that we stop and pay attention to a
lily, to just one lily. The wonder is that this can be done every day by
every one of us.

We hear a lot about the longing for spirituality. Even politicians tell us
that their surveys show that lots of people have this longing. Spiritual
longers.

At the same time we hear that many people are actually searching for
spirituality. Spiritual seekers.

The delusion created by such thinking is that the spiritual is out there
somewhere, either embodied in some person, or belief, or movement, or up
on a mountain, or deep in some forest, or even in some church—to be
longed for, searched for, sought out. Most of us are distracted from the
truth of any experience by such delusions and become lost in them. It's
possible to create a whole fiction of our lives, one that goes very far from
the spiritual center of things. And we have to work very hard to get back.

This can make the difference between taking things for granted and
appreciating them. When we look away, out there, into the future, we
naturally ignore what's here, right before us, right within us, every day,
every moment. Even if it's something unpleasant, isn't it better to ac-

knowledge and address it, rather than skip over it or move away from it? Are we prepared only to accept reality when we like it—and even then, just taking it for granted as if we're entitled to it? Or are we ready to appreciate it, knowing that whatever it is, it's given to us?

A teacher in the Christian tradition was once asked whether he thought he would go to heaven when he died. He said he never thought of such things, they had no interest for him. The interviewer asked rather sternly how this could be, since the belief in heaven was central to his religion. The teacher said that he had no idea what would become of him after he died, except that he knew he would be in God's hands. But, he added, he was in God's hands *now*, so he figured it would all work out.

What then are we longing for? What are we searching for? And where is it?

It is not in some imagined "out there." It's here. In *just this*. When we hear God's injunction to "go out," stated so beautifully in the story of Abraham, we may think it means literally to go out somewhere—to a mountain or a desert in the old days; to India or Tibet more recently. But it doesn't mean going anywhere. It means being here. Going out of the delusion and into *just this*.

But there are two good reasons for this misunderstanding. First, *just this* is often suffering, misery, pain, and torment. And secondly, "out there" is often a very pleasant fantasy.

> *And one day, as he was setting out, a man*
> *ran up and fell on his knees before him,*
> *and said, "Good Rabbi, what must I do to*
> *gain eternal life?"*
> *And Jesus said to him, "Why do you call me*
> *good? No one is good except God alone.*
> *You know the commandments: do not*

13

> murder, do not commit adultery, do not
> steal, do not bear false witness, do not
> defraud, honor your father and mother."
> And the man said, "Rabbi, all these I have
> kept since I was a boy."
>
> And Jesus, looking at him, loved him,
> and said, "There is one thing that you lack:
> go, sell everything you have and give to
> the poor, and you will have treasure in heaven;
> then come and follow me."
> But when he heard this, his face clouded over,
> and he went away sick at heart, for he
> was a man who had large estates.
> And Jesus looked around at his disciples and said,
> "Children, how hard it is for the rich
> to enter the kingdom of God. It is easier
> for a camel to go through the eye of a needle
> than for a rich man to enter the kingdom of God."

This story refers to the great "out there," the fantasy of material wealth. It may be money, or land, or political power. Or it may be a sexual fantasy, or an exaggerated interest in food, or just a belief that this is *our* world, that everything revolves around us—and especially around *me*. It is a very pleasant fantasy. One could even say that this is the central fantasy, the main distraction. The story of Adam and Eve in the Garden, one of our primary myths, centers on the strong temptation within us to make the world "mine," to control it all, to possess it. As the story shows, when we yield to this temptation, we begin living in a world of our own making, not this world. We become distracted from this world, the world we can experience moment by moment just by stopping to pay attention, and we become lost in another "world" of which we ourselves appear to be the center. Living there results, as the story of the Garden goes on to reveal, in alienation, then fear and shame, and eventually war against the rest of creation.

In that story of Jesus, the man is offered the opportunity to let go, to give up what he'd been holding on to. In general, the story is a response to the tale of Adam and Eve. Just as we are tempted and yield to the temptation to be in control, to enter the delusion, and to become alienated, so we can free ourseves by giving up control, by giving in to our own experience, by being just who we are, now, here.

No wonder we don't want to pay attention to *just this*, when *just this* reveals to us, as attention to the lilies reveals, that even the great Solomon in all his glory was not arrayed like this one flower. And *just this* isn't always a flower. There is a story in the Zen tradition of a man pursued by tigers until he is trapped at the edge of a steep cliff. When he looks down, there are more tigers below. He tries climbing down the cliff, and ends up holding on to a branch growing out of the cliff's face. It is only a matter of time before he isn't able to hold on any longer and falls to his death, to be torn apart by the tigers. He looks into the crevice from which the branch is growing and sees a wild strawberry. He picks it and eats it. It's delicious! . . . But sometimes there is no strawberry, and *just this* is just pain, or just loneliness, or just suffering, or just terror, or just being torn apart.

This is a good time to stop again. Close your eyes. Take three deep breaths. Relax. Now bring your attention to the rising and falling of the breath as it occurs naturally. Don't try to breathe in any special way. Just focus your attention on the breath as it is. Gentle, spacious attention. Noting lightly when the mind wanders. Gently and without judgment bringing your attention back to breathing. To the experience of the singular rising of this in-breath, to the experience of its unique movement, to the experience of its ending. To the singular falling of this out-breath, to its movement, to its ending.

Now, with a more focused mind, reflect on the awareness that both the desire to stay out there in the material fantasy and the aversion to staying right here in the unpleasant reality are driven by the same delusion: that this is "my" world, that it revolves around "me." This is the grand delusion. We don't have to climb a mountain or stay in a desert for forty days and nights or go to India or a church to free ourselves of this delusion. All that's necessary is to pay attention to *just this*. And remember, whatever it is, no matter how wonderful or terrible, it is nothing more or less than this.

# HAIKU MEDITATION

*Old pond*
  *a frog leaps in*
    *water's sound*

This is the classic haiku poem, written by the Japanese haiku master, Basho, a long time ago. It is about a moment—just the experience of this moment—"splash!" Every haiku is an attempt to reveal, in poetic form, such a moment, no more nor less. Often the first two lines set the scene, giving the reader a context. Then in the next line the poem opens to offer a moment of insight. True haiku are carefully created so as to lead to a "splash" that sets off ripples of thought in the reader.

This book is built around forty-four haiku, arranged by season. As you encounter each haiku, we recommend that you use it as a source of meditation. Begin by taking three deep breaths. Focus your attention on the experience of breathing in a natural rhythm. Stay with it for a while as you relax into a meditative state of mind. Then turn to the haiku and read it silently. Then read it again out loud. Read it yet again out loud. Then go back to the first two lines. Let yourself cross the threshold of awareness offered in those lines. Allow images, associations, feelings, memories to arise within you. Then move into the rest of the poem and allow yourself to be open to where it takes you. For the poet, it represents a particular moment of experience as well as his or her insight into that experience. Allow yourself to be open to your own experience, in response to the poem, and to your own insight.

Stay with it, and read the poem again. See what wider ripples it sets off in you. You may want to memorize it, and take it with you through the day to see what insights will arise.

As you read this book, you are invited to stop and give time to each haiku in this fashion, as a way of settling into your own awareness of what it evokes. Notice that just as the meditative exercise you've been practicing centers on what the body does naturally—breathing in and out—so the simple art of haiku is a measure of just one breath in poetic form. The breath breathes itself—in and out. All we are doing is paying attention to it. The world of the haiku is there before us; all we have to do is open the door to it.

We offer our own responses to these forty-four haiku to give a sense of how you might approach them in your own meditation. At the end of the book, though, we provide a few more without any commentary as an opportunity for you to meditate on them on your own.

# Summer

*Summer solstice—*

*half in, half out of water*

*a small frog*

The first day of summer. Things are changing. Things are always changing. If there is any one truth about existence as we experience it, it is that everything changes. As spring moves into summer, so the small frog becomes a bigger frog. He has no choice. He may like it in the water or he may prefer being out, it doesn't matter—along with all of Nature, he is moving into summer.

In the Buddhist tradition it is said that the Buddha taught us how to become free of the cycle of life and death. First he reminded us that suffering results from attachments. Then he said that attachments can be released through "mindfulness"—through being fully awake to the truth of things. When all attachments are released we live beyond the cycle of life and death. Does this mean that we won't grow like the frog from small to big, won't be half in and half out of the water, won't live within the round of the seasons, the cycle of Nature? Not at all. Like the frog, we will come into existence, we will change in form, we will be subject to the elements, we will be cold in winter and warm in summer, and we will pass out of existence. But by being completely awake, completely mindful, we won't be attached in the mind to any of it.

The warmth of the sun on one's face on the first day of summer . . . just the warmth on one's face.

So the *idea* of birth and death, and the constellation of ideas that is built on that idea, are released through mindfulness, through paying attention to *just this* as it arises and fades away. Most especially, what is released is the attachment to the notion of a fixed and permanent self. As that attachment is loosened and released, as each experience of "self" is seen to be no more than a chrysalis which we fill with ideas but which itself is essentially empty, the idea of the birth of a self and the death of that self is also released. We move from having taken our life into our own hands to realizing that we are always in God's hands.

This appears to be the central lesson of the Christian story of the resurrection. Jesus wasn't wounded and killed and then, with the blood barely dry on him, walking around three days later. That would just be a superstitious folktale. If one reflects on it, the story of Jesus teaches that as we let go of attachments, we yield our idea of a self, and so then die *into* life.

Do you feel more relaxed as you open your mind to the vastness of awareness? Can you see that everything floats free?

*Billowing clouds—*

*on her wedding gown*

*light and shadow*

The billowing clouds are beautiful, floating across the blue sky. But they do block the sun, and so on the similarly billowing and beautiful wedding gown we see both light and shadow. As it is in life, so it is in marriage. There is wisdom in the calling of the marriage vow for a commitment to each other and to the marriage "for better and for worse." When you come to think of it, it's amazing that we commit ourselves to such a vow —it's unique. And it seems not at all amazing that so many disavow marriage, given what it takes to live up to that vow.

Marriage may be understood to be a spiritual practice through which one yields, with anger, grief, despair, and finally acceptance, one's precious, private self to the greater reality. One's relationship with one's spouse, then, is not primarily personal, or even interpersonal, but transpersonal: an opportunity to free oneself from the suffering of selfishness.

The sky may be clear, then a few puffy clouds appear. Things change. Better put, everything has within it the potential for change. There can be no clear sky without the potential for clouds, no clouds without the potential for a clear sky. Life is made up of contrasts. Even on a sunny wedding day, there are clouds or the threat of clouds. Light and shadow.

The wish for an all-good, shining white world is a child's wish. But our adult conscience knows that there is no purity without violation, no union without alienation. It requires courage to live fully as adults, to die into life as it is—into *just this*.

Have reservations arisen in your mind, criticisms, doubts? As you quietly note them, notice how they dissolve. Can you feel the lightness of liberation?

*June morning—*

    *hands of the school clock*

        *skipping*

Time is moving. Nature is moving. We are moving. It's summer! Everything within us is moving in pace with Nature. And children naturally long to be outside, skipping.

They want to skip school for the day, for the whole summer! But the school clock is regulating time. The time on that clock is only moving one way, and all of time there is reduced to seconds, minutes, and hours, each segment a guidepost on a linear journey around the same circle, over and over.

There is tension in the way children live this June morning. From within, in response to summer all around, arises the urge to go skipping —down the path, through the woods, across the meadow, along the beach, even on the sidewalk of a busy street. But their summer is still regulated by that clock. The urge to become a skipping-away part of summer is contained by the requirements of that clock. In the great longing to be deregulated, is it their hearts that are skipping or is it the hands of the school clock?

Does this haiku bring you closer to a sense of freedom? Let yourself settle into the experience of breathing, the moving in and moving out of your chest or the way your abdomen rises and falls. If your mind wanders, note the sort of wandering it is—thinking, bodily sensations, judgments, memories—and then without judgment gently return to your breathing.

*Summer sun—*

*under the rhododendrons*

*yellow cat asleep*

Are you stopping for each haiku? Repeating it to yourself, then out loud? Are you giving yourself the time to enter the poem, to drop into its context, and then see what arises?

Here is a haiku without a person in it, or even the implication of a person. So taken are we by our fantasy of a self—"I," "me," "mine"—by its importance, by its independence, by its permanence, that we usually contrive to translate what's simply there into a story about ourselves; to interpret the idea of a frog leaping into an old pond in ways in which *we* are always central; and, ultimately, to translate the fact that the great reality around us seems to be beginningless and endless into *our* being immortal ourselves.

But why not accept *just this*? Just a yellow cat asleep—the laziness of summer. The roundness of the yellow cat like the roundness of the summer sun. The coolness of the shade under the thick-leafed rhododendrons. This is a haiku observation: a momentary experience of Nature as it is. It's selfless in the sense of being not self-conscious. If there is an implicit being observing, that being is in tune with just this moment in this natural world.

Are you aware of a lightness as you practice keeping your mind concentrated and open? Are you noticing the thinking mind? Isn't it amazing how active the mind can be—judging, explaining, interpreting, and just mulling things over? As your mind becomes alert, focus on the experience of thinking; gently and without judgment note this "thinking"; and then return your attention to your breathing. Can you feel the relief as the burden of self-reference is removed?

*Low tide—*

    *last night's dream*

        *fading*

When we are asleep, unconscious, a sequence of naturalistic and symbolic images forms. As we awaken, and our awareness shrinks back into the habits of consciousness, last night's dream fades. Deep awareness gives way to the well-worn path of wakeful knowing. It's as if we're standing on a beach, in the surf, and can feel the strong pull of the sea going out. As the water recedes and drags against us, our feet sink into the land. So, on waking we become rooted in our consciousness, all the time knowing that there is much, much more to this. Just as we may try to hold on to the receding tide, so we may try to hold on to the fading dream, the elusive images in it. But we can't quite grasp it as it fades. We feel as rooted in daytime consciousness as we are in the sand. And yet we also feel pulled by the power of the tide toward something, something we know, and yet something we fear to know.

Auden, in the poem "In Memory of Sigmund Freud," called on us "to be enthusiastic over the night, / not only for the sense of wonder / it alone has to offer, but also / because it needs our love."

We know the water will surge back, and our feet will be loosened, just as we know we will sleep again, and dream again. We know this cycle, far beyond our control, at times terrifying, ultimately consoling.

As you meditate, using these haiku as a means toward liberation, can you feel the constraints of the habits of consciousness loosening? Is it becoming easier to allow, like Freud and Auden, what has been exiled for so long to serve enlightenment now, with love?

*Summer afternoon*

    *last notes on the music box*

        *dragging*

A lazy summer afternoon, and the heat has drained the energy out of the day, just as the last notes are dragged out of a music box. The nostalgia of that old music box brings with it memories of a time of pure leisure, slowed down to a peaceful languor by the summer's heat. Listless, we can sit in the warm shade and feel the gentle breeze inviting us to do nothing but just sit here. No one is out and about—it's just too hot. Everything is still, unable to move. But everything is full—the trees at their leafiest, the grass at its thickest, the bugs at their busiest, and flowers everywhere. It is at moments like these that we can meditate on the shapes of clouds, on the receding boundary of shade and sun, on the industry of ants. We are slowed down, and it is a great opportunity to enjoy the feeling of being slowed down. In this state of mind, without any distracting energy, we can be at one with everything around us. In our slowed-down breathing, too, we can be at one with this summer afternoon. Nothing to be done.

As you slow down, here and now, whatever the weather and the season, are you more aware of what usually passes without notice? And are you aware, as you simply watch each phenomenon as it arises and fades away, of the restlessness of the mind, of the desire to get up and do something? Without criticism, simply note the restlessness and return to the rhythm of your breathing.

Or are you just aware of the laziness in the mind, a refusal to look more deeply, maybe an urge to go to sleep? It's okay—just stick with the practice of becoming aware, and gently note this interesting instance of laziness—and then return to the actual experience of breathing. Try to follow each of the tiniest movements of the breath as it rises and falls. Bring yourself very close to the experience.

*Moon*

*in the tide*

*with mother's ashes*

Notice the rhythm of the haiku: how it matches the rhythm of your breath. "Moon/in the tide." As you gently ease the words into the experience of an in-breath, allow yourself to be immersed in the setting of those first two lines. Then, as you follow the out-breath, allow the rhythm of "with mother's ashes" to carry you along to a moment of haiku insight.

The life of the self comes out of the Self and returns to the Self in a universal tidal movement. The moon is maternal, the generator of tides in their monthly cycles. And the sea in which the moon is reflected is the water between mother and child.

Along with the moon, a mother's ashes are being drawn out to sea in the ebbing tide. So, she herself is being drawn back into the fullness of life.

The whole cycle of life is contained in this movement. *Just this* contains everything. All we need to do is stop, breathe, pay attention.

*Summer heat—*

*every string on the violin*

*out of tune*

It's just too hot! Every string is out of tune, and nothing sounds right. The fiddle is useless now. One can't play anything in harmony. Better just to put it down.

In our "open 24 hours" society, every moment is advertised as a time to be active, to do something. But sometimes nothing should be done, or even can be done. This is the time to put things down and rest. With so much conditioning, with so much pressure, with so much desire, it requires a special effort to stop. The oppressive heat of summer helps us make that effort. When we try to play the violin in this heat, everything sounds wrong. At first we're annoyed, but as one string after the other goes out of tune, we become frustrated. Finally we can only laugh and surrender to the heat, to the season. In laying the violin aside, we're making peace with ourselves.

Strong impulses can arise in the mind—desire, hatred, fear, restlessness, laziness, doubt. Sound familiar? These are natural impulses, and as we accede to them, they hinder awareness and hamper freedom. Sometimes, even seeing these impulses clearly, and quietly noting the experience, doesn't affect their strength. When we try to refocus on our breathing, for example, within seconds the hindrance has arisen again. Often lots of these hindrances arise together despite our best efforts to concentrate. This is the time to laugh, lay it all aside, and rest.

*Among these lilies*

*in Monet's pond*

*Basho's watersound*

Here's that splash again, only now it brings together the spontaneity of Nature—Basho's "watersound"—and the art of a painted garden. Even in a pond as beautiful as Monet's, filled with a mass of lovely water lilies, the frog still goes "plop!" The splash breaks through the stillness of the art.

Now might be a good time for you to take a good look at Nature—the clouds in the sky, the tree outside your window, the ant crawling on your windowsill. Study what you see. Let your heart be open to the moment. Can you see the beauty in it?

Are you aware of the strengthening and deepening of bare concentration on the experience of the moment? And are you aware of the softening and opening of your heart? Now might also be a good time to include the practice of "lovingkindness" in your meditation. Close your eyes, take a few deep breaths, and get comfortable. Bring your attention from your breathing to your heart's center. Allow yourself to experience the breath now as it moves through your heart. Then silently begin to wish yourself well, using the phrases: "May I be happy. May I be peaceful. May I be free from suffering. May I be safe. May I be healthy. May I live with the ease of well-being." Then repeat the phrases, bringing your attention very close to the words. So, when you say "May I be happy," direct your attention deep into what it means to you to be happy. Continue to repeat the phrases for a while with the spirit of wishing yourself well. As your mind wanders, gently bring it back to the phrases. Notice how as you go on doing this, your concentration becomes stronger and your heart becomes softer. Enjoy this opportunity to wish yourself well, remembering that happiness *is* available.

*Night game*

    *the home run hitter*

        *tries for the moon*

Black sky, full moon, summer night. The millions of insects that fly unseen in the dark of any summer's night now revealed by the field lights. The white uniforms against the green grass. The excitement of a daytime game at night.

This is a sandlot game, and the players—our neighbors—are very close by. The score is tied, the crowd is tense. The pitcher delivers. Our slugger gives it his all and hits the ball high into the dark night. It's flying toward the moon. What a moment! It's perfect—everything in alignment—our emotions building to a crescendo, the drama of the pitch, the crack of the bat, and then the white ball sailing into the black sky, heading for the moon.

Living entirely in this moment, totally involved in the game, we travel with the small white ball flying into the vast black sky. Does any insight arise? Perhaps a growing awareness of the floodlit ball field as a tiny patch of light in the limitless darkness. There is a sense of awe. We may realize that this pitch, this swing, this hit are tiny aspects of a beginningless, endless, interconnected web of being, in which everything—including that ball in space—depends on everything else. As our hearts open to this mystery, we may struggle with certain feelings of dread, of inadequacy, and confusion. The boundaries of the old story, the one in which we are central, give way to a recognition of the way things really are. This dread, this inadequacy, this confusion—these are only fantasy feelings in a fantasy self struggling to lay claim to something much greater, something entirely selfless.

Note gently in yourself "a fantasy self struggling."

# Summer into Autumn

*After the abortion*

*the rain all day*

*on the daylilies*

Returning home, exhausted, moved by waves of grief and then relief and then grief again. Sitting in the window, alone now, staring. Suddenly, out of the blue it begins to rain. There is an emptiness, a blankness as the raindrops fall and streak down the window. Is the mind empty or just numb? There is a spicy smell from the soaked garden. In the stillness, can we hold and hug ourselves? But there is no consoling us now, only this solitary staring.

Out there is a clump of daylilies—one that actually bloomed before the rain began. Now, the force of the sudden, steady downpour tears at the delicate blossom. Pieces of the lily, meant to be a glorious sight, have fallen to the ground. Today is this flower's only day to bloom. Yes, tomorrow there will be others, but this one only has today. And today is not a good day to come into this world. This lily won't have another. There will be no second chance to show itself, to be itself.

Can we still wish ourselves well, even on a bad day?

If we see a field mouse running for its life with a hawk circling overhead, should we wish the field mouse well? On hearing our good wishes, that mouse might say: "Well, thanks, I guess, but those wishes can't help me now." The hawk might then add: "Yes, after all, I'm only being a hawk." And we ourselves might ask: "How can these wishes do any good, when there's nothing I can do, or even should do, to stop the inevitable?" To which we might reply: "We can't stop the life force as it goes where it will, creating and destroying. It's too great. Yet we can still wish ourselves and all beings well in the midst of it all."

Even on a bad day, we can still open our hearts.

# Autumn

*Monarch flyway*

*over the dunes*

*a long orange ribbon*

We are sitting on the sand among the dunes. Summer is ending, though the sand is still warmed by the descending sun, and the water is warmer than it's been all year. We look up and see a few monarch butterflies, half flying, half swept along by the breeze. We look again, down over the dunes, and see a long orange ribbon of butterflies. We're moved by the wonder of it, this trail of color and movement. Those thousands and thousands of little insects on their flyway, traveling thousands of miles. It's a wonder and a mystery to us, as we squint to follow this wonderful design stretching far beyond.

While you follow the movement of each breath, doing it as gently and carefully as if you were cradling an infant in your arms, notice that each tiny aspect of an in-breath is followed by another tiny, spontaneous aspect. Then notice that just as the last aspect of the in-breath ends, the first tiny aspect of the out-breath begins. And the next, and the next, until the last moment of this out-breath fades. Then notice there is a pause before . . . the first part of *another* in-breath appears. Like that long orange ribbon, our breathing is one new experience linked to the next, each separate, each unique.

Like the season changing, like the butterflies migrating, you too are changing, out of compassion, one tiny aspect after another.

*Harvest moon—*

*their wedding rings tucked away*

*one inside the other*

On this cool autumn evening the harvest moon
seems so close, so golden, so personal. And look,
it's surrounded by a luminescent ring. This mysterious
sight—the moon nestled in its ring—evokes a certain tenderness in us, a
softness of the heart.

It reminds us of wedding rings, tucked one inside the other. Perhaps a
loving tribute to our grandparents' marriage, begun when they were just
teenagers and ending only with their deaths. Or are these the discarded
rings of our divorced friends, once so in love and now so at odds that only
the rings have found a way to be together? Or are they the rings of the
young couple who will be married next week, waiting to be exchanged as
symbols of love and hope?

Sometimes when we begin to practice meditation, we have a hard time
accepting that it is basically doing nothing—just paying attention. Even
this isn't like paying attention to a teacher in a schoolroom—"Will this be
on the test?" Rather, it's relaxing in the knowledge that we are always free
to do it, that it just comes naturally when we let go of everything else in
the mind. We are so used to setting goals and working hard to meet them
that we can tighten our concentration to the point of getting a headache.
We're so used to suffering to gain merit that we can just persist, ignoring
the message that the body is sending us: "It's okay. You're trying too hard.
Relax. Allow yourself to open up to what's there. Everything else will take
care of itself."

As we open up to the mystery of things, as when looking at that harvest
moon in its ring, our hearts may fill with a mixture of feelings: pleasant
remembrance, poignant sadness, and hope. All are there.

*Indian summer—*

*someone blowing on*

*the embers*

The butterflies are long gone now, the sun is on the wane, the leaves are falling. Yet the wonder and the mystery of life continue. Suddenly, in the midst of autumn we wake to what seems like a summer's day. Indian summer. The fire seemed almost out, but someone blew on the embers. We can feel a last flush of heat from it. For a few days anyway we set aside our coats and hats to enjoy that last warmth.

The Buddhist meditation teacher Sharon Salzberg has emphasized that practicing meditation is like planting seeds. All we have to do is sow them. The dharma—the natural process—will take care of the rest. So, as we practice, we can let go of the illusion of control and become carefree. Just noting the experience, just bringing our attention back to each breath. Just saying the phrases of lovingkindness from the heart. We can lean into the dharma, and have faith in the mystery. One day so hot we give up; the next so cool we know winter is coming; then, a warm day amidst the falling leaves.

Along with blizzards and hurricanes, Indian summers remind us that we aren't in control. No need to try to control meditation. No way to come up with the right answer. Just keep your attention focused on the experience. Whatever there is to learn will appear. Is your heart soft, your mind open, and your awareness gentle and spacious, without judgment?

*Leaves*

    *yellowing*—

        *school buses*

Nature turns to the cycle of autumn: children leaving behind the playfulness of summer and the wild greenness of it all to return to the routine of school. The powerful innocence of Eden, of childhood, of summer, gives way to the conventions of schoolroom knowledge, of growing up. The leaves, once tender buds, then vibrant green shade umbrellas in the summer sunlight, now, as the light fades, are separated from their trees.

In the process of developing a discriminating mind, grounded in awareness and compassion, we realize how many cares are based on irrational fears. So conditioned are we to identifying with those fears, we feel reluctant to simply see them for what they are and let them go. At first we can't quite believe that we can live free of so many cares, we're so accustomed to the burden. How will we be thought of if we are actually happy? What will we think of ourselves? For so long we have actually given ourselves credit for being so careworn, as if we were one of the few who took it all seriously.

The wonderful message of the Buddha is that we can be free of all the cares that come with anger and grasping and fear and doubt. Then we can be free to care about what really matters—the happiness of all beings.

Now may be a good time to come back to the practice of lovingkindness. Begin again by drawing your attention to your heart's center and wishing yourself well, silently repeating the phrases: "May I be happy . . . peaceful . . . free from suffering . . . safe . . . healthy . . . and may I live with the ease of well-being." Now expand your good wishes to include a person who has been very good to you in your life, saying: "Just as I wish to be happy, may you also be happy"—and so on. Allow these heartfelt thoughts to embrace the other person. Remember, when the mind wanders, as it will, bring it gently back to the phrases.

*Autumn rain—*

*among the marigolds*

*a rusty key*

A darker time is coming. Autumn rain is always more serious than spring rain, somehow more ominous. Things have been dying off for a while now. Yet even in this cooler, darker time the last of the marigolds are holding on to their rust-colored blooms. As rusty as . . . what? This old key in among the fading flowers. It's a surprise, a bit of a mystery. Whose key is it, and for what use?

The insights that arise in the course of meditating are often surprises. The awakening mind lets go of the old fictions we invent and opens to the plain truth of what exists. But this is a process and sometimes, as we let things be rather than trying to manipulate or control or interpret, a mystery arises. We experience the mystery—it can be both delicious and unsettling. So we note the experience and then focus again on each breath. Meditation teaches us to expect nothing; everything will be opened to us.

*Autumn moon—*

    *at the anniversary*

        *a white chrysanthemum*

For the Japanese, white is the color of death. So much of Nature is dying in autumn, and here is a white chrysanthemum to commemorate this anniversary of death. Above, the great white autumn moon, like a great white flower in the sky. Below, a single chrysanthemum, bowing to the moon in reverence for all this dying away.

Or is it a wedding anniversary—the romance of the autumn moon reflected in the beauty of one white flower? Is the flower perhaps a gift, an anniversary present? Does it commemorate all the years of flowers, each one a year of marriage, recalling the passionate spring of its beginning, or the enlightened autumn of an older love? . . . Or does it just reflect the gentle light of the moon?

As our concentration develops, as awareness deepens, as our hearts soften, we bow to all the beauty and generosity around us. Look! Three goldfinches by a stream! When they flutter their little yellow wings they look like flowers trembling in the breeze. And look! That person stopping her car till I pull out of the driveway! Generosity.

The Buddha once came before a group of disciples to offer a sermon. At the end of the discourse, he picked a single flower and held it up for all to see. One of his followers, Mahakashyapa, responded with a knowing smile. Buddha's deepest insight was transmitted to him "Mind to Mind"—without conceptual thinking.

Thoughts drop away as we let ourselves relax, dropping deep down from the inevitable agitation of the individual mind into the Mind immanent in just this moment.

*Twilight—*

    *the autumn hills*

        *give up their colors*

A simple awareness of autumn in the evening.

We acknowledge the grace with which Nature gives up all the brilliance of its colors, surrendering itself again to the never-ending fullness of life, as twilight fades into darkness, toward winter.

This time is sacred. If we're sensitive to it, it takes our breath away. And as we begin breathing again, we're aware of the movement of our breath—coming in and filling us with energy, flowing out peacefully into the world. No effort.

We observe the way in which Nature around us gives its self, dying, to its undying Self. We become aware, just by taking stock, that we needn't make any special effort to give ourselves over to something greater. We are doing it all the time. As David Steindl-Rast said, Jesus didn't tell us what we must do in order to be saved—the good news he reminded us of is that we are already saved.

In everyday language, this means that, despite our delusions, we have never really left home. The breath breathes itself, moving in, moving out, the chest rising and falling. At twilight, the autumn hills give up their colors.

When we meditate—slowing down and taking stock—we can begin to be truly aware of the natural rhythm of life and death, and rebirth and redeath, and so on and so on. Then, as we look more deeply, we find ourselves letting go of life and death, and seeing *just this*.

*Low clouds——*

*with a vengeance*

*I weed the mums*

The dark clouds of autumn are low to the ground. There is a threat in the air, but it hasn't rained yet. There is an intensity throughout Nature. The heart is as heavy as the air.

What is needed is a simple task. The garden is still full of the remains of summer's wildness. Weed the mums! The garden will profit, the weeds will suffer. All of this pressing down needs a release. To clear the air.

As you reach for the weeding tool, are you aware of the movement of your hand and wrist and arm? Are you noting, in a gentle, transparent way: "reaching"? Just reaching.

As you press the tool into the earth beneath the weeds, can you feel the tension in your arm and shoulder? Are you holding the moment-to-moment experience in your mind—openly, gently, clearly?

As the heaviness in the air builds, can you feel the bodily sensations of this tension—in the head, around the eyes, in the throat and chest, throughout the body?

As the weeds are uprooted with a vengeance, as the air clears, as the heart finds release, are you staying open to just this experience? Without thinking. Without analyzing. Without interpreting. Just this experience of the heart's release. . . .

*Snapshots scattered*

*in a drawer—*

*the autumn wind*

In the relentless, ever-changing experience of moment after moment, we take snapshots. They are attempts to hold outside time's flow certain captured moments of one's life. Here they are set against the autumn wind, which blows hard already, and will lead to the even stronger winds of winter.

We've set the snapshots aside, put them in a drawer. We try to hold on to these photographed episodes in our lives, to preserve them. When we look at images of ourselves, of others, of places, we remember now how we imagine it was then. Was it a happy time or a sad one, a time of promise or of resignation? "That was me," we say. "That's the way I was then." But is it true?

While we sit looking at these snapshots, we can feel the autumn wind, hear it. Nature won't let us stop life, capture it, hide it away. When we hear the wind whistling through the shutters, we're learning from Nature that our plan to record and preserve things is a fantasy, a waking dream.

What it tells us is that we have to let go of the "me" we've made an elaborate mental catalog of—the imagined character in that story we take to be permanent, independent, real. As our meditations deepen, and increasingly we find that so much that we'd thought was real can be abandoned, our hearts become more open to ourselves and to all around us. How little we actually need, how much we can give without any effort, how much easier life is than we had thought.

*Anemone petals*

*how darkly*

*they fall*

Now, late in the year, the trees have lost their color, the wind is blowing, it's colder and darker. We bring the flowers that normally bloom in spring inside our hothouse. In doing so, we're trying to supplant Nature's way with our own, trying to swim against the tide, even stem the tide.

Yet even as we sit and contemplate this captured beauty—a pot of anemones—suddenly and silently, without any warning, one of its petals drops. Just like that. And the dark reality of it sinks in.

At a moment of deep insight like this, the mind often escapes again into yet another story, another fantasy, another waking dream. The dark reality of it challenges our greatest attempt to supplant Nature's way: our clinging to a belief in our independent, permanent selves. When lost in that delusion, we'll do anything—even kill ourselves, kill others, kill everybody and everything—to maintain that dream.

It has been said that at its best meditation is a process of grieving, through which everything, all of what we treasured and all of what we loathed, falls away, like the anemone petal.

# Autumn into Winter

*Rain*

    *changing to snow*

      *last goodbye*

As the rain changes to snow, we say goodbye. We grieve as we accept the reality of this change. We bid farewell to the apparent, which we'd been clinging to. We yield, give up the fantasies and attachments. It is a last good-bye.

Yet we know that under the snow-covered ground the roots and bulbs are growing. In the spring, what died will live again, the same again and yet not the same.

So there is a goodbye to all that's been, which, paradoxically, is final and not final.

Meditation—just paying attention with an open heart—teaches us how we love. This can be especially true when what we love is passing, is dying. Was our love of certain flowers an openness to the beauty of their form, an affection for their fragrance and color, a delight in their gentle swaying in the breeze? As the petals shrivel and fade, as the stems bend to the ground, as the leaves brown, can we let them go? Or do we long to hold on to them, to defy their nature and possess them? There may be a bit of both in our loving—the grasping of desire and the yielding of lov-ingkindness. As desire and lovingkindness each arise, we can ask our-selves: which results in anger and suffering, which results in generosity and freedom?

# Winter

*Morning frost*

*expecting her voice*

*I unlock the door*

Loss.

After a loss, it takes a long time for it to sink in, to sink in to the heart. Nature is saying: it's over, but for us humans it's hard to accept. The clear, natural truth can't be accommodated easily in our hearts. Even when, with considerable difficulty, we can release our wishes and desires, and even when we can surrender our accustomed way of living, still there are attachments. Are they ever fully released?

Now would be a good time to do a lovingkindness meditation that includes a close friend or family member. Begin again by wishing yourself well, using the familiar phrases. Take your time. Release the words from the heart, and keep your attention very close to them. Happy—peaceful —free from suffering—safe—healthy—living with the ease of well-being.

Stay with yourself for a while. Then, when you're ready, extend the circle of good wishes to a benefactor. Enjoy wishing this person who has been good to you well.

Then, when you are ready, open the circle of warmth to include a dear friend or family member of whom you're very fond. Enclose that person in those heartfelt phrases. Move from yourself, to the benefactor, to the close friend or family member. Allow your concentration to deepen, the lovingkindness to build.

At any point, open your awareness to the quality of love you're sending to your loved ones. Is it freely given? Does it ask nothing in return? Does it accept the ways of the other person?

*First snow*

*on the wings*

*of cemetery angels*

The trees are bare now. The cemetery is dark, all grays and browns. The white snow on the gray stone angels' wings highlights the somber colors of winter. As the first snow falls, we are aware that what was alive is dead. Nothing is left, all has passed. Only the cemetery angel marks the spot.

Wings—the means of flight, the way of resurrection, the feathery symbol of hope—are stone cold, heavy, weighed down by snow.

This is a dark time, and it will become darker. The first snow announces that winter is upon us, and there will be a lot more snow. The power of winter and of death inspires a sense of awe in us.

At some time in our experience of meditating we come to a "dark night of the soul." Without our realizing it, the cold fog of doubt permeates our minds so that we refuse to accept that what we experience is real. Instead we tell ourselves a story, a story of doubt, in which nothing really matters, in which all our meditative efforts are useless, in which suffering is without release. This story seems to be comforting for a while, but it ends in despair.

So now, we gently open our minds to our doubt, our despair. Not as concepts but as actual experiences. And as we concentrate on them, they may lift, float up and go. Out of this liberation may come a respect for the power and majesty of winter.

*Winter wind*

*blowing leaves over*

*sparrow's bones*

The winter was too much for this little sparrow. It froze in the cold, lay there on its side, and decomposed. Only the bones remain. Now the leaves, long dead, are blown by the winter wind over all that's left of that once airborne life. Desolation.

In the spring, when these leaves are raked, nothing will remain.

"Poor thing," we think, when we come across a bird's bones on an icy path. "Poor us," we feel, linking our sympathy for the dead creature to ourselves, wishing we could somehow stave off the power of the winter wind.

Can you hear the story developing in your mind? Can you feel the temptation to identify with that self-centered story? Now is when the seeds you planted through meditation practice should come into flower, now in the depths of winter. Now is when mindfulness should remain steadfast. Note the story as it arises and, without any attempt at judgment or correction, gently focus again on your breathing.

Out of this may arise the insight that in wishing ourselves and all beings well we cannot control the way things are. We're trying to open our hearts to what is, to *just this*. In that spirit return to your lovingkindness meditation. Focus your attention once again on the heart's center. On the words: "happy . . . peaceful . . . free from suffering . . . safe . . . healthy . . . living with the ease of well-being." First wishing yourself well, then extending it to a benefactor, a close family member, a beloved friend. And why not sparrows, too?

We can't expect to harness the power of winter. Instead, we can practice opening our hearts, so that we can observe and experience this winter wind, these dead leaves, these bones, and even this nothingness, with detached compassion.

*Urban sunrise*

*the garbage truck brakes*

*heave a sigh*

The sky is just beginning to lighten on this dark winter morning. We awaken to the sound of the garbage truck's brakes. We sigh in response, turn over, and sigh again. Outside, the truck, braking again and again as it goes about its appointed rounds, echoes our sigh back over and over.

Another morning! From the garbage truck to sleepy wakers throughout the world, it's all the same—we all have to get going again. We all have to truck that load. The whole world heaves a sigh: "Here we go again!"

When we wake up, before we truck out of bed—especially on a cold, dark morning—can we begin the day with the practice of lovingkindness? Wishing ourselves well: "May I be happy . . . peaceful . . . free from suffering . . . safe . . . healthy . . . living with the ease of well-being." Opening the circle of good wishes to a benefactor, to an intimate friend, to a close family member. Enjoying the experience of deep breathing as we lie there wishing ourselves and others well.

And what about that garbage man outside in the cold? To you he may be a "neutral" person—someone you see from time to time, maybe say hello to, but don't really know. Include him in your round of good wishes. Along with yourself and those who mean a great deal to you, include this stranger. Bring the image of his face to mind and, using the phrases, wish him well. When you do this regularly, you may be surprised to discover how much this "neutral" person, this stranger, has come to mean to you.

*First snowfall*

*the table set*

*for one less*

The first heavy snowfall is a striking signal that things are really on the move again. We're now heading into a much colder time.

We awaken to a world turned white and the sudden realization that something important has happened. Everything is buried in snow. We aren't going anywhere today. It's distressing to have our regular schedule disrupted—everything out of sync—and yet it's a relief to surrender to this greater power.

As we sit and watch the snow fall, we can feel our breath rising and falling in our chest. We're still here, alive, and much of our world is intact; but something significant has changed. We are being reminded of our place in the world. The raw power of the wind and snow is as natural as the gentle movement of our breath.

Death and loss and grief are natural, too. Someone who belongs at the table is no longer going to be there. In setting the table this time, in carrying out that routine task, we automatically expect things to be as they always have been. Suddenly, we become aware of the difference: the table now must be set for one less.

The new table setting, like the first snowfall, signals something we've already felt in our hearts—a displacement. There is comfort in accepting the truth, but there is sorrow, and anger, and fear too. The weather has changed, the situation has changed, and in our hearts we are changing too. Surrendering to what is real. Letting go of our fantasies. Suffering through the change emotionally. Tolerating, and finally accepting, the way things are. Releasing so much to find ourselves feeling okay at this table set for one less.

*Winter morning—*

*the closet dark*

*with old shoes*

We awaken to a chill, dark January morning. Probably better to stay in bed—there's a strong urge just to pull the covers over our heads—but we have somewhere to go.

We pad around in the dim morning light and stumble into the dark closet. Inside it are all those old shoes, shoes that have gone so many places. Even in the winter darkness we can see in the shoes parked side by side on the closet floor the paths our life has taken.

"So," we might reflect, "this is where they've taken me—to a cold room in the dark of winter! I wonder where they'll take me next."

As our mind focuses and our heart softens, we can calmly inspect whatever comes before us. Without fantasizing, without letting any hindrance to bare attention distract us, we can see clearly what's there and then *into* what's there. In this case, a bunch of old shoes in a closet. As we look at each pair we see how they are shaped, how they feel, how they smell. And more deeply, where we have been in them, and who we have been. What at first was just an old shoe becomes a companion, a vessel of memories and emotions, a source of quiet laughter.

*Snowdrifts getting deeper*

*what do they mean—*

*my dreams*

A serious snowstorm. We are snowed in. Long ago we gave up the idea of going anywhere, and now are sitting inside on this winter's day, watching the snow pile up, layer upon layer, covering everything. As the snow gets heavier, it weighs down the shrubs, and the trees become ghost-like figures. Everything, coated like this, becomes strange, shrouded, just as our dreams, when we try to recall them during the day, are strange—weighed down with layers of meaning, holding secrets within.

There is such a dream-like quality to snow as it falls heavily and piles up, tranforming our regular world into an uncanny landscape. Sitting here, watching it, one feels the urge to remember what is underneath, just as when waking from a dream.

Sometimes it isn't easy to see into what is there in front of us. We know that our dreams are just ways we have of telling ourselves about ourselves when we are asleep, and yet we have learned to keep from ourselves so much of who we fully, truly are that our dreams seem strange. Amazing, isn't it? What we tell ourselves about ourselves must be told with so much secrecy and arcane symbolism that we can't remember it, and if we can, we can't understand it. At such moments our inner world seems shrouded, muted, alienated, as the natural world seems when it's covered with snow.

Isn't it sad to realize that we have learned not to accept who we fully are? And isn't it wonderful to remember that gradually, with courage, we can come to accept and include even what at first had appeared so strange, so horrible, so not-me in our dreams?

Can we be resolute about facing, with bare attention, the reality of things? Even when we discover that the old narrow myth of who we are no longer holds, and the emerging, fuller person is so unexpected?

*Winter sunset*

*in the coffin she wears*

*her fanciest dress*

The sun sets so much earlier now, and seems so much more precious. We go out into the descending darkness to be closer to the vanishing sunlight. As we stand in the cold wind, we notice the contrast between the almost gaudy sunset and the bare, gray trees. This earth seems dead beneath that lively sun-show. When the light in the sky fades completely, we turn away, into the black winter night. What was that glorious display—and why?

The old lady in the coffin took her vanity to the point of absurdity by saving her fanciest dress for the last. Does it matter?

We live so long in love with ourselves, wanting to be loved by others, and troubled by this or that problem with me and you. Yet at the same time we long to release the burden of self, recognizing—deep in ourselves—that we are small potatoes in the big picture, and that what we can know, even at our most brilliant, is only a profoundly limited vision of what is there.

So, can we ever free ourselves from this sometimes glorious, sometimes horrible, sometimes burdensome feeling that we are somebody, or ought to be? Or do we all conspire secretly to wear our fanciest dress in our coffins? After all, even a sackcloth, or no cloth—even believing that only the soul lives on—even believing there is no self—is a way of clinging to our sense of importance. Otherwise, why would we go look at the sunset—and write about it?

*Starless night—*

*my rearview mirror empty*

*I sing the blues*

There are times when you are immersed in the sadness of the moment. There's nothing ahead of you and nothing behind you, just a sad song that comes welling up—the blues. For that moment nothing else exists for you. You are just there with it, with your true feeling, singing.

This isn't a hopeless feeling, because you're not looking at anything ahead or behind. There's nothing for hope or hopelessness to attach to.

You're just giving voice to the sadness of the moment, and there's even something joyous then about singing the blues.

This would be a good time to continue with a lovingkindness meditation. Focus your attention on your heart. Then envelop yourself, a benefactor, a good friend, a family member, and a neutral person in good wishes, using the familiar phrases. Once you get into the rhythm of this, extend the circle of good wishes to include a difficult person—someone who has hurt you, someone you fear or hate. Go slowly. Don't try to talk yourself into wishing that difficult person well. Don't try to deny your feeling of fear or hate. If it gets to be too much, return to yourself and your friends. When you are ready, try the difficult person again. Remember: you aren't trying to change that person, only to open your heart.

Are you like the man who held a grudge against another man for years? Every time he thought of the other man he felt anger, hurt, and resentment. One day he sat down and cried for a long time. As he cried, he thought of nothing. There was no past or future. He just cried, and in that moment he was sadness in human form, nothing else—and so felt relieved, released, and joyous. In his mind the words arose: "Why did I wait so long?"

Are you aware of holding on to the past, or projecting into the future, as if it were real? Try gently noting in yourself a "memory" of a "fantasy," and then returning to the experience of breathing. Forgiveness is simply letting go of the weight of a state of mind.

89

*Sparrow chirping—*

*this winter morning*

*its white breath*

Look up at that frozen branch on this icy morning. On it is a sparrow with its feathers all puffed up, fluffing the air between the feathers to protect itself from the cold. The little bird's breath is visible—just a puff of whiteness. What joy there is in it! This sign of life on a dark, cold morning takes our own breath away.

As our awareness deepens with practice, we find our breath being taken away more and more by the ordinary experiences all around us and within us. Nothing special—just a tiny life expressing itself—singing!—in winter's frozen world.

Now allow a lovingkindness meditation—opening your heart and sending good wishes—to be available to all beings as they arise in your awareness. Open the circle of goodwill to include yourself, a benefactor, a friend, a family member, a neutral person, a difficult person—and now, all beings. Start with all beings as only abstractions at first, and then bring them into your heart. Feel free to focus your wishes on all men and then all women, then all beings below the water, on dry land, and in the air. Let yourself go. And as any being comes spontaneously into your mind and heart, embrace it with these good wishes.

Noticing a sparrow on an icy morning, wish it well—"Just as I wish to be happy, peaceful, free from suffering, safe, healthy, and living with ease, may you also be happy."

# Winter into Spring

*Snow*

*changing to rain—*

*crocus tips*

This one-of-a-kind snowflake is melting into a unique raindrop. The season and, with it, our mood is changing. The cold breaks, the darkness gives way to light. The snow melts, and the raindrops are tears of release.

New birth. Up through the wet snow, resurrection. What was dead is alive again: just the tiniest tip (no flower yet) of hope and trust coming up again out of the snow, out of a dead time.

Are you still struggling with wishing that difficult person well? Don't worry—it's okay. There can be no policy or prescription for affairs of the heart. Sometimes when the image of someone who has harmed us comes to mind, we just can't feel warm toward that person. Our heart is wintry. Do you know those days when the heart is cold, hard, and closed? There are such days. But sometimes, with practice, the mood of lovingkindness will well up in us. A deep sob may come, and then the release of crying. The relief is so sweet that those words "Why did I wait so long?" may also come. But there is no timing forgiveness. Like the crocus tip it has its time.

Yet it's a good question: why did I wait so long? Maybe the question itself is the beginning of an awareness that, as the Buddha has assured us, there *can* be a release from suffering, and that release can be realized through mindfulness and compassion. Isn't that right?

# Spring

*First day of spring*

   *a robin hops over*

      *the last smear of snow*

During the last, lingering days of winter, as we pace around inside looking out at the snow and ice, we find ourselves checking the calendar more than once: when is the first day of spring? But whatever the numbers may say, it's the abrupt arrival of the first robin that tells us that spring is finally here. When that jaunty little bird hops over the last smear of snow, we cross over with it into a whole new season—a new attitude.

There is, of course, romance in the idea of spring: the sap is rising, the brook is running, the sun is turning in our direction. But at a deeper level there may be a sense of vague unease at the sheer speed of it. Like that bird—here, and . . . hop . . . now there. What was snow a moment ago is now a puddle, a bird's play pool.

And we may realize that we're not just witnesses to all this but participants. The truth, if we're willing to gaze steadily at it, is that *nothing* is permanent. Everything breaks down, dies, and decays. Everything is reborn, develops, and flourishes. We may value, even romanticize, one arc of this cycle—the one that's young and vibrant—but the cycle is relentless.

Slow down, allow yourself to settle into a close awareness of the ongoing, endless process of birth and death, and to experience these moment-to-moment changes. Does fear arise in response to it, the thought "And what will become of me?" Now is a good time to address this thought, and then quietly shift your attention back to your breathing. It, too, you notice, is changing. Where, you may wonder, in all these transformations is there anything stable that might be called "me"? Then, calmly and maybe with a bit of humor, recognize that you may actually feel at ease with the experience of impermanence, moment to moment.

*Filling the leafless*

*pear tree with gold—*

*migrating finches*

It's still early spring, the branches are still bare, and we can't expect blossom and leaves for quite a while yet. So—what a nice surprise! Today about a dozen little finches landed in the tree, like little, plump, golden pears. Nature's preview of what is to come.

The birds are there only briefly, stopping to rest. In a few moments, they are gone, moving on. And the tree is left bare again, waiting. (Saint Augustine said that while he was out and about looking for God, God was always there in his heart, waiting.)

Like the tree, the mind is empty. There is nothing there intrinsically, permanently, and independent in origin. Into the emptiness, like finches into the tree, come thoughts, feelings, judgments, sensations, intentions. We might say these experiences are migrating. They have an origin that is dependent on conditions here, there, and everywhere. Yet there appears to be an order to the way the experiences arise and migrate. We call this apparent order "karma." Yet who can know the vastness and complexity of the workings of karma? Out of the whirlwind, in response to Job's questioning, came the response: who are you to ask?

Bring your mind to bear on this one day, this one place, this one moment, when finches fill the leafless pear tree with gold. Is your mind quiet, is your heart open, to be moved by the beauty of just this moment? In early spring, before its time, this tree is full of pears—then, all of a sudden they're gone! Can you be open like this to what passes thro mind and heart?

*April sunrise—*

*baby discovering*

*her fingers*

There is a delicious Middle Eastern dish called Imam Bayaldi, or "The Priest Fainted." The story is that a Muslim priest was invited to sample this dish, and was so overwhelmed by the taste of it that he fainted. There is a similar moment in the Zen story where a monk, walking down the street in a large American city, looked up, saw a flock of Canada geese migrating, and fainted with joy.

Do we need to be priests or monks to have these experiences? Not at all. In fact, we are exposed to them all the time. All that's required is that, like the priest and monk, we pay attention. But how do we do this?

"April sunrise": it is an April morning, and spring is in the air. Are you paying attention? Are you aware of the coolness against your skin? Of the night's dampness? Of the faint, rosy horizon? And then of the golden streams of sunlight, enlightening the world? Of the joy in the heart over these experiences, available in an ever-changing form *every day*?

Once at a sunrise Easter service in a Benedictine monastery, after hours of praying, singing, and lighting candles in the dark, the doors of the chapel were swung open to reveal the April sunrise. The priest didn't faint, but he did dance. And then he led one and all around in a circle, a dance of joy and unity.

In a way, every day is Easter. The sun rises every day. Not in any special way—it's just here, *just this*.

Jesus said that unless we accept the kingdom of God like a child we cannot enter it. *Enter* it. It is here, right here, and it is to be entered. In our delusions we are outside it, lost in our thoughts and beliefs. It is here just as a baby's fingers are here. Right in front of us. Part of us. We can't miss it. All that's necessary is that we pay attention, just as the baby is paying attention when she discovers her fingers—are they part of her, or is she part of them?

Gerard Manley Hopkins wrote: "There lives the dearest freshness deep down things." Deep down things. The challenge is: how do we see that "dearest freshness"—not in the morning sun in a monastery, or even through our bathroom window tomorrow morning—but on a very, very bad day? We must look—deep down. We must stop to look.

Take three deep breaths. Bring your mind to bear on the natural movement of the breath. Notice once again that it moves of its own accord. It isn't our breath, my breath, it's *the* breath. Now look again. Is the mind racing, are the emotions churning, is the body pulsating? Note the racing, the churning, the pulsating. Then gently bring your mind back to the natural rhythm of breathing.

103

*Early spring*

    *a mother and child draw*

        *their family tree*

In early spring we venture back into the garden. When we were there last, before the ground froze and the snow covered it over, we found ourselves thinking about the hosta leaves. Bright and green and hardy last spring, then tough and thick and full last summer, then a solid green backdrop to the mass of stems and purple flowers in the fall. By winter they had become yellow and brown, parchment thin, spread out against the ground, giving up their last moisture.

Now the soil has thawed but is still cold, and there is no trace of last year's hosta. But as we clear the debris of winter from the garden, our fingertips touch the firm, tiny yellow shoots of this year's plants, breaking through the loosening soil.

Then, when we look back at the house, we see a touching scene—a mother helping her child to figure out who came before them on their family tree.

Are these tiny heads of hosta the same hosta that died back into the earth over the winter? No. Are they completely different? No. Spring is always new, always a reincarnation of all that came before.

The child delights in knowing that she has the same name as her great-grandmother. "Who was she, Mommy? What was she like?" asks the child. "She was my mommy's mommy," answers the mother. "Oh, let's begin again!" shouts the child.

*Plum trees—*

*in white dresses*

*young girls*

Begin again. You can always begin again. Gently close your eyes. Allow your attention to settle on your body. Feel the warmth of the body. Feel the heaviness of the body. Feel the contact of the body with the chair and the floor. Gradually, become aware of the movement of your breath. Narrow your focus. Focus on the experience of the in-breath. Focus on the experience of the out-breath. Focus on the contact of the lips, one against the other, during the pause between the out-breath and the next in-breath. Keep your attention on just this in-breath, and on just this out-breath. Now bring it even closer, to the experience of the rising of just this in-breath, and keep it there, closely, gently. As your mind settles on this experience, an insight may arise: that there are just these moments, forever rising and passing away.

Plum trees in bloom, against a clear blue spring sky, each blossom newly opened. The air still cool, the sun gaining strength. Young girls walking arm in arm, in their new white dresses.

Gazing at the plum trees and these girls, we are touched by their newness, by their fragility. If only we could stop time. Yet tomorrow or the next day, when we go into the garden, those lovely petals will be on the ground, no longer fluttering in the breeze. The air will be warmer, the sun stronger. That wonderful moment, like the in-breath and the out-breath, will be over, and a new moment will be arising and passing. Just as the girls will soon be young no longer, their white dresses no longer new, their laughter echoing down the pathways of memory and soon silent.

So, each of these moments is precious. Each is like the lily of the field, arrayed in all its glory.

By practicing meditation we don't learn that we should do this and not that, obey these rules and not those, follow some special way and not another. Rather we are invited to see things anew, as they are, and once we do, we will naturally live in a way that is dedicated to happiness and freedom, for ourselves and for everyone else. When we bring the mindfulness and compassion we have developed through meditation to the sight of those flowering trees, how could we pollute the air and soil and water out of which they grow? When we see those girls from that point of view, how could we not want to shield their fragility with our strength, and treasure this fleeting moment of their youth?

*April breeze—*

*rereading*

*love letters*

Allow your eyes to close gently, and bring your mind to bear on just breathing, being attentive to the experience of the in-breath and the out-breath. Now check to see that your mind is open, clear, relaxed, alert, and without judgment. If it isn't, open your heart to whatever it is. Accept it sympathetically. Let go of a commitment to change through judgment and criticism, and open to change through compassion.

Whatever we discover about our shortcomings as we meditate, however we find ourselves distracted by what the Buddha called the hindrances —desire, aversion, restlessness, laziness, and doubt—can we care for ourselves as Jesus and the Buddha care for us? Can we evoke the Christ within us, our Buddha-nature, and allow our hearts to tremble with compassion as we see clearly how we really are?

After the real death and the apparent death of winter, Nature stirs with the first warm winds of spring. The rereading of love letters evokes the same renewal of feeling, the stirrings of remembered love. Spring is the rereading of life, and the April breeze is a coming back to life. T. S. Eliot wrote that April is the "cruellest month," perhaps because however set in our ways, however closed our hearts, the reawakening in April is painful, and irresistible. As Nature opens up, the warmth of April thaws our hearts, exposes us to all the vulnerability and fallibility that being fully alive entails.

Rereading love letters is a thawing, too. The old pain of strong feelings revives. Hard as the earth has been, it must crack, soften, and yield to what Dylan Thomas called "the force that through the green fuse drives the flower."

An April breeze of awareness helps remind us of our wintry ways, how hard set we become in our delusions about the importance of "me" and "mine," how intent we are on staying outside the Garden, in a world of our own making. And old love letters, too, help remind us of our wintry hearts.

*Light rain*

*a sprinkle of arpeggios*

*from the street musician*

Art and Nature: the music is in delicate harmony with the rain. There is a playful give-and-take about it—a sprinkle of rain and a sprinkle of notes. When we feel the drizzle, we are pleasantly aware of the delicate connection between ourselves and Nature. When we hear the shower of music, we enjoy the connection between ourselves and art.

Each haiku is a little work of art, calling up through its images and energy certain associations—the memory of being sprinkled with rain, of hearing a spray of music, of seeing a street musician. The heart is softened and the mind is lightened by these memories. As we note the memories and prepare to return to the experience of just breathing, can we give a deep sigh and relax, so that when we come back to our breathing again, it's with the softness and lightness evoked by the poem?

Notice how haiku and meditation are both focused on just the everyday, naturally occurring experience. Every moment, every experience is an opportunity for attention, insight, and enlightenment. Sometimes we may think that only great events have significance. Or, in despair we may feel that no event, nothing, has value. But when we slow down, really slow way down, and pay attention with an open heart and a mind free of judgment, we awake to the fact that every moment matters—this one and this one and . . .

*Just before dark*

*the cardinal's song*

*brightens the pine*

By gently focusing your attention and generously opening your heart, little by little, again and again, a meditative mind will develop. But what is a "meditative mind"?

A man, strolling by the river, hears and then sees a rainbow trout leap through the air, and is so staggered by the grace and beauty of it that he leans against a tree. A woman, going for her evening walk, sees the full moon that has been hidden by clouds for a week, and bursts into tears, saying: "I missed you!"

Meditation is the experience of being alone with yourself. It takes quiet and solitude just to give your mind a chance to calm down. What better place to enjoy your own company than here, along a forest path at dusk, amid the coolness of the late spring as the sun sets through the trees, the fragrance of the pines, the softness of the moment.

Out of the stillness comes the silvery piping of a solitary bird, a cardinal. Your mind, the meditative mind, has been practicing for just this moment: your care in attending to the subtle experience of breathing, your efforts toward opening your heart to everything you can.

Calm, alert, compassionate, you're amazed at the cardinal's song— and for an instant, though you never see the bird, the pine tree in which its nest is hidden lights up.

Once you have had this experience, can you see that the idea of a "meditative mind" is extra? Only that instant—the sudden song and the brightened pine, the moment you were open to—existed . . . and then was quickly gone. But you can always return to it, as a confirmation of your meditation practice and an inspiration to continue.

Now, don't you find that you can attend to your breathing and your heart again with renewed enthusiasm and commitment?

*Daytime moon—*

*up from the subway*

*a bag lady*

Sometimes, looking up into the vast, empty sky in the middle of a bright, sunny day, we are surprised to see the moon—a "daytime moon." What is the moon doing up there in full daylight? We expect it only at night. Suddenly we're reminded that the moon is always there, always in its place, day and night, but we feel it doesn't belong. It's unsettling to realize that we have made up an order of things that isn't the true order.

Seeing a bag lady coming up from the subway into our world is much the same. We are reminded by her appearance that, like the moon, she is always there. We aren't used to seeing her, though—not in our daytime, above-ground world. She carries bags around with her—junk—our junk—junk that's also always there. She carries poverty, carries madness, carries desperation around with her. Like it or not, the sight of her reconnects us with the real world, in which we are all interconnected.

We try to live in our own personal, inner worlds. We try to live "above ground." And then a "bag lady" comes up from our unconscious "subway," and we are challenged by the awareness that everything is related. Knowing this is at once comforting and unnerving; knowing that, like the daytime moon, all of it is always there.

Deep down we know that this is a broken world and that we are broken, too. Often, though, we try to get fixed, or pretend everything is fixed and all right. We try to change in response to censure and so we yield to a narrow, constraining, even oppressive experience of ourselves and of the world. But through lovingkindness meditations, through the compassion we develop, we can learn to accept that we are broken and still love ourselves, that this world is broken and still love it.

The deeper the meditation, the more frightening it can be. There will be other bag ladies coming up from the subway. But if we keep our minds open and our hearts soft, we can accept whatever arises as what is truly here and now—*just this*.

*First morning glory—*

*girls telling*

*secrets*

Once the Dalai Lama was being interviewed outdoors on a summer day, and both he and the interviewer were being distracted by mosquitoes. Given that Buddhists believe that one shouldn't harm any sentient creatures, the interviewer asked him what he did about mosquitoes. The Dalai Lama smiled and answered that it depended on how he was feeling on any particular day. When he woke up with an open heart, full of a sense of fellow-feeling, and a mosquito bit him, he felt he was simply being a blood donor. But when he woke up feeling cranky or distracted or irritated, then he blew the mosquito off gently before it could bite him. When he woke up with a closed heart, he was just annoyed by the mosquito, and flicked it off. And then, in his inimitable manner, he turned to the interviewer and asked: "Is that right?"

So, the heart opens and closes.

The wonder of the morning glory is that it too opens and closes. Similarly, girls open up and close to each other. In that special time of childhood, girls open up entirely to their girl friends and confide in each other. Then, like morning glories, they close, and these confidences become secrets. Like the treasure in a locket, their confidences take on great value.

We are all "girls" when we are open. This is what in the Zen tradition is known as the "beginner's mind." At those times, there is a freshness to us, like a flower fully open to the world around it. Then, in the mysterious rhythm of opening and closing, just like the morning glories, we close. Our breathing opens and closes. Our heart opens and closes.

Sometimes, when trying to open our heart, the most resistant, closed, and difficult person can be ourselves. We can become wracked with worry, guilt, and self-hatred. We try to wish ourselves and others well, but these good wishes are sent in a context of anxiety and remorse. After a great deal of psychological and spiritual tossing and turning, we might congratulate ourselves on being finally free from hating others, yet still we are aware of hating ourselves. In our struggle to wish ourselves well, suddenly we might have the insight: "You know, right now you are such a difficult person!" We might even sit there and sob. We might feel horrible for all the harmful things we've said and done in our lives. There's no hiding from it all.

Then, a voice might arise from somewhere inside us and say: "I love you." And we will cry, really cry, but now out of relief and a deep gratitude. We will feel lucky, knowing that despite who we've been and what we've done, we can still hear that voice.

Like the morning glory, the heart cannot open when it isn't ready, and we cannot stop it from opening when it is. Meditation is the practice of preparing for the opening.

# Spring into Summer

*Long ago*

*I would have picked*

*these violets*

The days are getting longer now. Walking along, looking down—there at our feet is this lovely clump of violets. Surprised by their color and beauty, we stand before them. And we remember how many times as children we would have picked clumps of violets like these, wanting to possess them, without thinking. How many times did we pick a handful of them, carry them around for a while, and then leave them to wilt on the grass?

Now, all we want to do is enjoy them, be in their presence, and wish them well, letting them live as long as they can. As we've grown older, we have grown to see that they share this precious life with us.

Just to see them—that's enough! Now we can keep them in our mind's eye. No need to possess them. May these violets live out their own existence, moment by moment . . . .

*But why this need*
*to elaborate*
*the mystery*
*of all that is?*

*Is it not enough*
*and more*
*to leave it all*
*unmetaphored?*
*To simply name*
*and let it*
*be.*

*As here*
*in this patch*
*of violets, in this stone*
*and in the encompassing*
*silence.*

We hope that, by learning to slow down and pay close attention, you have come to some understanding of what meditation and haiku are all about, how they are expressions of the same intention: to see into a particular moment with compassion.

All of us, however fortunate, must live with suffering in this life. Even in a large, well-furnished home in a safe area, with lots of money and all the material pleasures, we are still subject to the natural disasters—fires, floods, tornadoes, blizzards, and earthquakes. We may be traumatized by social disasters—economic reversals, political upheaval, radically changing social conditions, and war. We are vulnerable to family discord, abuse, divorce, and abandonment. We may be involved in physical accidents, or suffer illness and disease. We will lose our loved ones, and eventually we will grow old, get sick, and die. For the less fortunate and the unfortunate among us, these difficulties are compounded by poverty, lack of education, unemployment, epidemics, hunger, war, oppression, violence, poor housing or homelessness.

Even when things are going well, we have learned over and over that even the most resilient pleasures won't last, that no appetite can ever be finally satisfied. And for all of us, behind all the pleasures and difficulties of life, there is the low but insistent hum of insecurity. We know that if we eased off from our need for distractions, the emptiness behind them would be revealed. What we see, when we do take the trouble to look carefully, is that everything is in flux, that we are not in control, and that the ultimate dynamic is a mystery.

If we hold steady and go on looking, we will see that it isn't the difficulties and insecurities in themselves alone that cause us unhappiness and suffering. Like all things, disasters come and go. If we aren't killed, we may be wounded. If we aren't destroyed, we may be broken. Sooner or later we can expect to be terrified, traumatized, ruined, abandoned, or heartbroken. If we are able to go on, we will bear the scars on us for life. The power of these difficulties is real. Trauma shakes our whole being, and yet it isn't the effect of having been so shaken that causes suffering. The ultimate cause is the self-centered story we tell ourselves about the actual experience.

In reaction to each passing episode in our lives—whether deliciously happy, or quite nice, or tolerable, unsatisfactory, or horrible—we usually tell ourselves a story which revolves around ourselves. And we get lost in that story. We fit it into the narrative we call "our life," the narrative we're so familiar with that we have come to think this is who we are. When the alarm goes off in the morning, sometimes even before we open our eyes, a story is already going. It may be the same one that came up yesterday and in just the same way. Hearing it again and again doesn't seem to stop it as we get out of bed. We can become so absorbed in it that we don't notice the warmth of the shower against our skin, the sound and unique feeling of water, the taste of the toothpaste, the birdsong just outside the window. The day goes on, the week goes on, the year goes on, our precious lives go on, and we live within these fictions as if they were real. When the alarm clock went off, we never woke up; we just went from one form of dream to another.

We can proceed through this waking dream of a life, not only suffering as we do, but telling ourselves and being told by others that this is the way it must be, and even that it's all for the best. We can become so captivated by it that discovering the impermanence and emptiness of it all can be not simply shocking, but terrifying.

Yet we all want to be free, and we all want to be happy. And—good news!—freedom and happiness *are* available. Right here, right now—*only* right here and now. Waking up and practicing staying awake to *just this* is the very experience of liberation. It is the way out of suffering and into freedom. Meditation and haiku are a means of waking from the dream, of letting go, of forgiving.

Not only is it liberating, it's also simple. Here we invite you once again to return to the experience of just breathing, alert to each breath, in and out, rising and falling. As you do this, you are invited to bring the same calm alertness back to each of the haiku we have responded to in this book, one at a time. This time, though, come to each of the poems anew, on your own. Don't read our commentary. Instead allow yourself to drop into each haiku, feeling the natural rhythm of the poem, letting yourself be drawn into the context and following it through to wherever it leads you.

In closing we offer you the following four haiku without commentary.

We hope you find them useful as you meditate.

*How free they are—*

*cherry blossoms falling*

*here and there*

*Scattering his ashes*

*the moon*

*in bits and pieces*

*How peacefully*

*darkness descends*

*on the water*

*Last words spoken—*

*I listen to the sound*

*of my breath*

## ACKNOWLEDGMENTS

We gratefully acknowledge our debt to the genius of Basho and his haiku followers in Japan, and to the spirit of R. H. Blyth, who first made the works of those poets available to us in the West. It is largely because of them that our eyes have been opened to "the haiku moment."

We are also grateful to our friends at the Insight Meditation Society, who shared their wisdom and experiences of meditation practice. We drew strength from the generous conversations and helpful comments of Sharon Salzberg and from the enthusiastic encouragement, during days both bright and bleak, of Joseph Goldstein. We also appreciate the kind support of Sylvia Boorstein at Spirit Rock Center.

To haiku teacher Tony Suraci, for incredible intuitive energy and an ability to draw the haiku essence from even the vaguest phrases, a special note of thanks. Deep gratitude to our friend, haiku poet Virginia Brady Young, who never wavered in her belief that our manuscript would one day turn into a book. Thanks also to Faith Middleton of Connecticut Public Radio for her optimism and encouragement.

We deeply appreciate the work of our inspired editor at Kodansha International, Stephen Shaw. His sympathetic readings and thoughtful suggestions were consistently to the point. Thanks as well to our illustrator, Noriko Murotani, and to Megan Kalan of Kodansha America, who has been helpful and a pleasure to work with.

Finally, our appreciation is immense for that ever-widening circle of haiku writers and readers in the Haiku Society of America and, indeed, around the world, and to all those for whom meditating has become a vital practice. To you we extend our gratitude and goodwill, and hope that our book helps to bring you inner peace.

# ABOUT THE AUTHORS

Photo: Ameen-Storm Abo-Hamzy

**Sylvia Forges-Ryan,** a former Editor of *Frogpond*, the journal of the Haiku Society of America, is internationally known for her haiku poetry, which has been published in numerous journals and anthologies and translated into many languages. She has won the R.H. Blyth Award, the Harold G. Henderson Award, the *Mainichi Times* First Prize, the Museum of Haiku Literature Award (Tokyo), and the Grand Prix from the Atomic Bomb Memorial Committee in Kyoto. She also writes and publishes in longer poetic forms.

**Edward Ryan** holds a Ph.D. in Clinical Psychology from the University of Michigan and is devoted to the study, teaching, and practice of psychotherapy. He is an Associate Clinical Professor at the Yale University School of Medicine and has a private practice of psychotherapy in New Haven. He is also a practitioner of insight and lovingkindness meditation and has served on the board of directors of the Insight Meditation Society.